The Feminism Fallacy

Rejecting the Errors of Feminism
and Finding True Womanhood Through Christ

The Feminism Fallacy

Rejecting the Errors of Feminism
and Finding True Womanhood Through Christ

☙

Ireland Gentry-Dillard

Foreword by Deanna Huff

RESOURCE *Publications* · Eugene, Oregon

THE FEMINISM FALLACY
Rejecting the Errors of Feminism and Finding True Womanhood Through
Christ

Resource Publications
An Imprint of Wipf and Stock Publishers
199 W. 8th Ave., Suite 3
Eugene, OR 97401

www.wipfandstock.com

PAPERBACK ISBN: 978-1-6667-5602-9
HARDCOVER ISBN: 978-1-6667-5603-6
EBOOK ISBN: 978-1-6667-5604-3

This book is dedicated to my parents,
T. J. and Amy Gentry,
who raised me in the Lord,
gave me the gift of writing,
and have always been my biggest supporters.

Contents

Foreword

The waves of feminism throughout the twentieth century have shaped the perspectives of many women today. The surface claims of equality between men and women appear to advocate for women, but Ireland Gentry-Dillard attests there is a better way. Sadly, some women today are attempting to uphold and carry out the view of feminism because they believe it to be the way home. Yet, as Ireland shows, the sometimes latent and often obvious fallacies in feminism's attempts to point a way home only lead to despair. In her pursuit of truth and support for women, Ireland unfolds the beauty and goodness of God's plan for women of every generation. She offers in this work a call to deeply think about the feminist agenda in light of the Bible.

In a substantive, though non-technical and conversational way, this book describes Ireland's personal journey and former desire to follow feminism's unfulfilling path. She celebrates God's original purpose in creation for men and women as integral to the complementary beauty of mankind. Recognizing that God's perfect design was altered due to the effects of sin which led to the power struggle between men and women, Ireland analyzes the basic claims of feminism and exposes their futile attempts to offer hope and meaning to women apart from God's loving plan. As she shows, the emptiness of feminism's claims led her to exit the feminist path and rediscover the road home for women along the way of God's truth.

You will enjoy this devotional style of reading that draws you to contemplate the ideas of feminism in light of the Scriptures.

The portraits of Jesus caring for women are filled with grace and guidance. The value of women emerges through the compassion of Jesus. The last few chapters will motivate the reader to self-reflect and ponder their views in light of the Bible.

If you desire encouragement toward the path of God or simply desire to further examine the feminist claims, then this book is for you. You will find her bold and compassionate style engaging, and you will be drawn nearer to the deep love Christ has for you. As you will see, Ireland is eager to equip women and help them grow in the faith.

Deanna Huff
Assistant Editor, BellatorChristi.com

Introduction

I BEGIN THIS BOOK knowing full well that there are many people who probably opened it to scoff at Christianity and its "antiquated" ideals. I realize that many will read this book either partially or in its entirety and either misrepresent me or disagree with me. I pray for another outcome, but I am a realistic woman.

If you fall into this category, then please hear me, friend: I was once a self-proclaimed feminist. I listened to feminist music, wrote feminist prose, threw myself into feminist literature, took every feminist English course offered during my studies and advocated for awareness to the cause. I've been offended by men who opened the door for me or insisted on helping me carry something. I've felt sorry for women who "just want to be stay-at-home-moms" and hoped they would one day be as enlightened as I once considered myself.

I was a feminist AND a Christian. If you identify as both, then I am not condemning you. Feminism isn't equivalent to apostasy. However, it is not the way God intended women to live, and I believe that God's way is the best way. Why would we want anything less than God's best? He created us, women. He created every facet of us, every nook and cranny, and he knows the hurts and desires in our hearts. Feminism will not heal those hurts or satisfy those desires. Only God can do that.

When my perception of feminism shifted, I did not quit my job. I did not stop writing, reading, speaking my mind, strengthening my body, or debating with men. I did not change my personality (bold, outspoken) to conform to some sort of "quiet" feminine ideal. Not at all.

I feel there are a few things you should know about me before we dive into this discussion:

1. I am a fifth-degree black belt in jujitsu. I am a sensei (licensed to teach the art) and I almost exclusively teach men. Sadly, not very many women feel confident enough to learn jujitsu. With that being said, I can defend myself against men in a fight. I don't see anything wrong with this.

2. I was educated in a secular university setting under strong, capable feminist and feminist-friendly scholars.

3. I am not a hoity-toity, strict and stern woman who is out to judge other women.

4. My hair is currently purple. Don't know if that helps, but there it is.

Still with me? I hope so.

Chapter 1

In the Beginning

Before feminism is addressed, we must first understand what it means to be a man and what it means to be a woman. Thus begins Genesis: "In the beginning God created the heavens and the earth . . . Then God said, 'Let us make man in our image, according to our likeness' . . . So God created man in his own image, male and female he created them" (*The Holy Bible NKJV*, Gen 1:1, 26–27). Notice how the Bible does not say, "Male OR female he created them." From the very beginning, God made two distinct and separate sexes with distinct and separate charges. Genesis continues:

> And the Lord God formed man of the dust of the ground, and breathed into his nostrils the breath of life; and man became a living being . . . And the Lord God said, "It is not good that man should be alone; I will make him a helper comparable to him." Out of the ground the Lord God formed every beast of the field and every bird of the air, and brought them to Adam to see what he would call them . . . But for Adam there was not found a helper comparable to him. And the Lord God caused a deep sleep to fall on Adam, and he slept; and he took one of his ribs, and closed up the flesh in its place. Then the rib which the Lord God had taken from man he made into a woman, and he brought her to the man. And Adam said: "This is now bone of my bones and flesh of my flesh; she shall be called Woman, because she was taken out of

Man." Therefore a man shall leave his father and mother
and be joined to his wife, and they shall become one
flesh. And they were both naked, the man and his wife,
and were not ashamed. (Gen 2:7, 18–25)

The Scripture is extremely clear: men and women were created for a purpose, and each purpose is unique. Adam was created not only to worship and enjoy the Lord, but to tend to the
Garden of Eden and have dominion over the land and creatures of
the earth. Because the Lord is a loving and good God, he desired
Adam's happiness and brought forth Eve as a helper to him.

Brace yourselves, ladies, because you might feel as though
you've rubbed up against a cactus, but here is the truth: the Bible
clearly reveals why God created women, and that reason is to help,
complement, and be enjoyed by men (in marriage). Does it feel
like you've been pinched, stubbed your toe, or smelled something
sour? I get it. It naturally causes us to bristle, but that is our sin
nature waging war against God's purpose for our lives by trick-
ing us into thinking that God does not have our best interest and
happiness in mind. Plainly put, we don't like the idea of being told
what to do, or whom to do it for. We want to do what we want to do
when we want to do it. But that is not why we were created, and it
is why the world is such a wreck. People are pursuing their desires
above all else.

Despite the heavy charge and trust Adam received from God
to have dominion over the land, he messed up worse than Eve did
when it comes to eating the fruit from the tree of the knowledge of
good and evil. Genesis tells us, "So when the woman saw that the
tree was good for food, that it was pleasant to the eyes, and a tree
desirable to make one wise, she took of its fruit and ate. She also
gave to her husband with her, and he ate. Then the eyes of both of
them were opened, and they knew that they were naked; and they
sewed fig leaves together and made themselves coverings" (Gen
3:6–7). We know that Adam was created for the initial purposes of
glorifying God and ruling the land, but he received an additional
purpose and duty when Eve was created: he was to honor, protect,
and lead his wife. When the time came for him to fulfill his duty,

he royally blew it. He didn't protect her and lead her. He allowed her to be deceived by the serpent, and he even indulged with her in sin by eating the fruit.

God confronted Adam and Eve, and Adam failed her once again. Instead of admitting that he had failed Eve, he shifted all of the blame to her: "Then the man said, 'The woman whom you gave to be with me, she gave me of the tree, and I ate'" (Gen 3:12). God was not unaware of Adam's failure, and that is why Adam received a more detailed punishment than Eve (and even the serpent):

> To the woman he said: "I will greatly multiply your sorrow and your conception; in pain you shall bring forth children; your desire shall be for your husband, and he shall rule over you." Then to Adam he said, "Because you have heeded the voice of your wife, and have eaten from the tree of which I commanded you, saying, 'You shall not eat of it': cursed is the ground for your sake; in toil you shall eat of it all the days of your life. Both thorns and thistles it shall bring forth for you, and you shall eat the herb of the field. In the sweat of your face you shall eat bread till you return to the ground, for out of it you were taken; for dust you are, and to dust you shall return." (Gen 3:16–19)

There is quite a bit to unpack here. We'll start with Adam's punishment. What once was effortless in the Garden of Eden (growing crops, gathering food, tending to the animals) would now be exhausting and at times nearly impossible. This is the result of God's curse on the ground. Because of his failure and sin, Adam would now be required to work hard and often without much to show for it. His life would be full of toil and frustration. He would be required to provide for his wife even though the labor was intense.

Now to Eve's punishment. The Lord said he would "greatly multiply" her sorrows regarding conception and childbearing. You should notice a couple of things about this. If something is being multiplied, it means that it already had to exist. Zero multiplied by anything is zero. Clearly God created women for childbearing as a primary purpose and duty. If Adam and Eve hadn't fallen, child-bearing would still have been part of God's plan: it just wouldn't be hard or painful (and sometimes devastating). It would have been perfect because the world would not be in its current fallen state.

There is something else you should notice about God's statement towards Eve. He said that her desire will be for her husband, and that he will be the one who rules over her. God did not say, "Your desire for your husband will be increased, and he will rule over you even more." By introducing the idea of desire as a punishment, God is saying that she would not have been in such a state if the fall had not happened. Desire is used here in the sense that Eve desired to usurp her husband's authority as head of the household, yet she must submit to him. Additionally, we can surmise that Adam would not have ruled completely over Eve. They would have been more like partners in the true sense of the word. After all, Eve was created so Adam would not be lonely. The Bible tells us that Eve was "comparable" to Adam. As a result of the fall, however, she was now subject to her husband whom she now saw as an incapable leader but was required to obey.

The subjection of Eve is a key element to understanding how we, as women, should respond to feminism. Do you think Eve enjoyed painful childbearing, relying solely on her husband, and having him rule over her? Probably not, especially considering she had previously been a co-inhabitant of paradise. But there are consequences for our actions, and we are all reaping what Adam and Eve sowed in the Garden.

Chapter 2

Defining Feminism

WHEN I SPEAK TO others about feminism, they often seem to regard the movement as "pro-woman." In fact, most women (and even men) I have discussed the issue with will openly proclaim themselves as feminists. "After all," a woman once told me, "it would be stupid not to be on my own side." I work at a college, and at a recent meeting one of my fellow professors (a man) had on a pink shirt that stated, "Women's Rights are Human Rights."

So is that what feminism is? A human rights issue? I considered his shirt as the meeting that definitely should have been an email droned on, and towards the end I decided that our society does, indeed, view feminism as a human rights issue. A quick search of the Merriam-Webster Dictionary online yields this definition: "Feminism (noun): belief in and advocacy of the political, economic, and social equality of the sexes expressed especially through organized activity on behalf of women's rights and interests."

A simple syllogism yields a similar conclusion: All women are humans; humans should have rights; therefore women should have rights. So, thinking back to my coworker's shirt (Women's Rights are Human Rights), the statement is not false. It's logically correct. Feminism is an attempt to advocate for and maintain human rights.

If this is where the definition of feminism ended, we could probably all agree with it, and I could stop writing this book. What started as an idea with good intentions now has a seriously flawed expression. The second half of the dictionary definition mentions "organized activity" to advance women's rights. One of the organized activities is advocation for abortion.

I never thought I would see the day where Roe v. Wade would be overturned—not because God couldn't do it, but because he often lets nations stumble and sin their way into judgement. I figured America would keep digging itself into a hole. Now, it still is—don't get me wrong. There are many states still performing abortions, but it is no longer considered a Constitutional right (nor should it ever have been, in my opinion). There has been a great uproar since Roe v. Wade has been overturned because the right to abortion has always been such an essential tenet of feminism.

Let's lay out the argument for abortion from a feminist's perspective:

An obvious human right is the control over one's own body. This is a free country, after all. People can choose to be overweight, be thin, tattoo themselves, cut their hair, wear makeup, not wear makeup, what to clothe their bodies with, when and if to go to the doctor, to receive or reject medical treatment, to risk their lives, or to even kill themselves. We are all free agents. Because of this, feminists believe that a woman should have the right to decide what goes on inside of her body. If she decides she does not want to sustain the embryo or fetus inside of her, that is her right to choose. No one should interfere, because it is her body, and she is the ruler over her body. It is her decision. Sound familiar? Of course it does. We are inundated with this ideology almost constantly. On the surface, it can be hard to refute, especially if you're dealing with a non-Christian. But more about that later.

Another expression of feminism is the recent #MeToo movement. #MeToo is a way to hold men accountable for the abuse women have suffered at their hands. Many celebrities spearheaded this movement and called out men in their industries who had sexually harassed or abused them at some point. I would bet that almost all women can relate to the #MeToo movement, hence its name. As I write this, I reflect on the times I have suffered harassment at the hands of men. I do not feel safe going places alone most of the time. I have been catcalled on numerous occasions. I cannot even mow my own lawn during the summer without my husband outside next to me—otherwise cars will stop, and men will try to talk to me, I will be honked at, and sometimes men will make crude gestures at me. All of this, mind you, while I am wearing no makeup, have my hair pulled back under a baseball cap, am dressed modestly, and have huge sunglasses on. Women are never "asking for it." I can relate to the #MeToo movement, and I am not condemning it. I think it has been (for the most part) a good way to hold men (especially men in positions of power) accountable. Take Harvey Weinstein for example—the once successful American film producer who is now convicted of rape and other forms of sexual assault. The #MeToo movement assisted in bringing his crimes to light. In a world where sexual assault often goes downplayed, ignored, or remains a secret out of fear, the #MeToo movement has given women the support and platform they need to hold men accountable. This is not where I disagree with feminism.

An issue that women still face today is what's known as the wage gap. The wage gap is a problem that has existed for years on end and is still, much to my horror, an issue today. Imagine being paid less for doing the exact same job as a man simply because you are a woman. Just the thought of it stirs up my judicial sentiment and makes me want to start picketing for change. Another syllogism reveals the egregious thought process behind the wage gap: A higher salary is the result of a competent and deserving employee; women are paid less than men; therefore, women are less competent and deserving than men. Doesn't this make your blood boil? Feminism seeks to address the wage gap by making others aware of it and advocating for change. Again, this is not where I take issue with feminism. The wage gap is a hideous reality and a definite mark of the world's fallen nature. I hope there will be change soon, especially since we live in a society that considers itself "woke."

Now that we've talked about many of the main tenets of feminism, you may be thinking, "Yeah, these issues are substantial. Feminism seems legitimate." Hold onto your hat. Although feminism touches on issues that are legitimately wrong and should be corrected, it also seeks to tamper with God's authority in other areas. The bone I have to pick with feminism has to do with issues that fall under this category, the first being abortion. Women, listen to me: we should not, cannot, and will not endorse any ideology that undermines the gift of life and the sacredness of the womb. Feminism claims to be pro-women, but what about the millions of future women being aborted at a steady rate?

As I write this, I am ten weeks pregnant with a little girl—yes, a daughter, a future woman who will have to wrestle with the concept of feminism at some point and will almost undoubtedly one day be able to relate to the struggles of women everywhere. She is one of the reasons I am writing this book. I want her to have a bright, Christ-centered future. I long for her to embrace her femininity. I am pained at the thought of the millions of babies who will not get this same chance because of the evil that is abortion.

Feminism is certainly not limited to the organized expression of women's rights. I'd wager that your average feminist does not partake in daily protests and the like. Your average feminist is just a woman who is trying to advocate for herself in the best way she knows how. I see you, I hear you, I feel you. I'm here to show you a better way.

Chapter 3

Man(kind) Has Failed

To begin this chapter, turn on Bonnie Tyler's song "Holding Out for a Hero." Go ahead. Permission has been granted. Blast it loudly. Allow yourself the inevitable foot taps and wiggles that will come with the beat. Let yourself relate to her when she sings, "Where have all the good men gone and where are all the gods?" She's asking valid questions.

If you take one look at this world, you will be able to see it is broken. Not just a little broken—it is utterly devastated by brokenness. It is so broken that we tend to hurt ourselves as we bump into its jagged edges and collide with other broken creatures wandering the earth. Sin pervades everything. So do we say, "Well that's just the way it is," and move on with our lives, groaning and stumbling alongside everyone else, resigned to brokenness? No.

Ephesians 2:10 tells us, "For we are his workmanship, created in Christ Jesus for good works, which God prepared beforehand that we should walk in them." God created us, and he created this world. God can do no evil—it would be completely contrary to the very core of his character, which is love. So if God created the world and its inhabitants, and God can do no evil, why is there so much evil in the world? Where, indeed, have all the good men gone?

I have often lamented the failings of men. Yes, men specifically. It seemed as though everywhere I looked, there were men mistreating their spouses, addicted to pornography, neglectful of their children, violent, lazy, cowardly, and generally weak. It turned my stomach and made me want to scream. For a long time, I kept that anger bottled up so tightly that it was such a cathartic release when I began to identify as a feminist and could finally call men out on their wretchedness. As I type this, I feel some of that old fire igniting within me, sparking my tongue and making me want to speak out.

But nothing will douse a flame quicker than a good helping of humility. We are ALL sinners. Yes, men have failed women, and they will continue to fail women until Jesus comes back again and sets the world to right. No matter—we have ALL sinned and fallen short of the glory of God (Rom 3:23), every one of us, male and female. Are the failings of men particularly painful and shocking? Perhaps at times, yes. But we are all sinners saved by grace.

Now, don't misinterpret what I am saying. Does this mean I think that women should continually forgive their cheating spouses, remain punching bags for men, and let rapists walk free, all in the name of grace? Absolutely not. There are consequences for sin. The Bible is extremely clear about that. What I am advocating for is that we do not let any root of bitterness spring up in us. Bitterness kills and destroys. Bitterness is a mark of the enemy. We mustn't become bitter against men. This is easier said than done, especially for women who have suffered at the hands of men.

There are instances of punishing men for violence perpetrated against women in the Bible. Let's recall what happened in the Old Testament when Jacob's daughter Dinah was raped:

> Now Dinah the daughter of Leah, whom she had borne
> to Jacob, went out to see the daughters of the land. And
> when Shechem the son of Hamor the Hivite, prince of
> the country, saw her, he took her and lay with her, and
> violated her. His soul was strongly attracted to Dinah the
> daughter of Jacob, and he loved the young woman and
> spoke kindly to the young woman. So Shechem spoke to

his father Hamor, saying, "Get me this young woman as a wife." . . . And the sons of Jacob came in from the field when they heard *it*; and the men were grieved and very angry, because he had done a disgraceful thing in Israel by lying with Jacob's daughter, a thing which ought not to be done. (Gen 34:1–4, 7)

Dinah was raped by a man who was overcome by desire for her. She was violated in the most intimate and horrific of ways imaginable, and there were many consequences that resulted from Shechem's sin. He would most likely not have been held accountable for his actions, while Dinah would bear the scar of his sins forever. Because she was no longer a virgin, she would be devalued and displaced unless she married her rapist. It was a blight on her and her family, all while Shechem roamed free. But Dinah's brothers had a strong sense of justice, and they made sure to avenge their sister:

But the sons of Jacob answered Shechem and Hamor his father, and spoke deceitfully, because he had defiled Dinah their sister. And they said to them, "We cannot do this thing, to give our sister to one who is uncircumcised, for that *would be* a reproach to us. But on this *condition* we will consent to you: If you will become as we *are*, if every male of you is circumcised, then we will give our daughters to you, and we will take your daughters to us; and we will dwell with you, and we will become one people. But if you will not heed us and be circumcised, then we will take our daughter and be gone." . . . And their words pleased Hamor and Shechem, Hamor's son. So the young man did not delay to do the thing, because he delighted in Jacob's daughter. He *was* more honorable than all the household of his father. And all who went out of the gate of his city heeded Hamor and Shechem his son; every male was circumcised, all who went out of the gate of his city . . . Now it came to pass on the third day, when they were in pain, that two of the sons of Jacob, Simeon and Levi, Dinah's brothers, each took his sword and came boldly upon the city and killed all the males. And they killed Hamor and Shechem his son with the edge of the sword, and took Dinah from Shechem's house, and went out. The sons of Jacob came upon the slain, and plundered the city, because their sister had been defiled. They took their sheep, their oxen, and their donkeys, what *was* in the city and what *was* in the field, and all their wealth. All their little ones and their wives they took captive; and they plundered even all that *was* in the houses. (Gen 34: 13–18, 25–29)

I'm certainly not condoning the actions of Dinah's brothers. They clearly committed mass murder in retaliation regarding Dinah's rape. However, the point is clear: rape, and any act of violence toward women, is inherently wrong and results in punishment. This has been true since the beginning of time. We are all, male and female, created in God's image. As image bearers of God, we must respect each other. There is a reason the Bible places such an emphasis on loving our neighbors as ourselves. Without this foundation, there is selfishness and suffering.

During Biblical times, there were even measures put in place to safeguard pregnant women. Exodus 21:22–25 states, "If men fight, and hurt a woman with child, so that she gives birth prematurely, yet no harm follows, he shall surely be punished accordingly as the woman's husband imposes on him; and he shall pay as the judges *determine*. But if *any* harm follows, then you shall give life for life, eye for eye, tooth for tooth, hand for hand, foot for foot, burn for burn, wound for wound, stripe for stripe." These are words given directly from God concerning life in the womb, which he clearly regards as precious. Once again, there are consequences for sin.

So, we've established that the world has been broken since Adam and Eve fell in the Garden of Eden. Things have always been bad, and they seem to be getting worse. As Bonnie Tyler laments in her song, "Where have all the good men gone?" Keep reading, friend, and I think you'll find that they are closer than you think.

Chapter 4

Redefining Feminism

We've explored the modern definition of feminism, and now it is time to redefine what it means to advocate for women as Christians. When the concept of feminism is rejected, I have noticed that others tend to think that the person rejecting it must be an old-fashioned jerk who thinks less of women. I'm sure there are some people out there who sadly hold that view, but I am not one of them, nor do I think the majority of my Christian brothers and sisters are.

Are there true aspects of feminism? Certainly. The desire to advocate for women is a just pursuit. My dad often says that "all truth is God's truth," meaning that we can appreciate parts of certain beliefs and ideologies without accepting every aspect of them. Why is this? If there is truth in something, the ultimate source of that truth is God. Others have just taken bits of his truth and skewed it. With that being said, we can appreciate certain aspects of feminism without accepting its errors.

I would like to begin this discourse by reflecting on the common behavior and energy of feminists. There is an air of arrogance in the self-empowerment of which they boast. Did that statement offend you? I told you this topic isn't an easy one to talk about. Allow your heart to be pricked as we delve into this subject, knowing that with each pricking comes pruning, and pruning is a blessing.

That's right—there is arrogance in the feminist self-empowerment often touted on social media and elsewhere. The ideas that women have everything they need within themselves to thrive, that they do not need anyone else to make them happy, that they can do everything that men can, and that their sexuality is their power are, simply put, poisonous lies. These lies are a way that the enemy attacks women and takes something that was meant to be good (the advocation for women) and perverts it.

Many women have bought into these lies. I was one of them for a very long time. I told myself I was whole as I was, and that I could do anything I wanted despite being a woman—no, BECAUSE I was a woman. This belief system ended in a breakdown in my physical and spiritual life. I was trying to be something I could not, and I was trying to pretend I was satisfied by deceiving myself. I would like to take you through the line of thought that eventually freed me from these chains by addressing some of the common attitudes and beliefs of feminism.

Idea one: Women have everything they need within themselves to thrive

This concept is attractive because honestly, who wouldn't want to be completely satisfied with themselves at all times and find every resource needed to succeed within? It's unsurprising that many feminists believe this, especially if they are not Christians or do not have a deep faith in Christ. Ladies, we, as Christians, should know that we absolutely do NOT have everything we need within ourselves to thrive. This goes for men too. If left to our own devices, we would quite literally self-destruct. We are sinful beings in need of a savior and the daily renewal of our minds. The only thing we're going to find within ourselves is an alarming propensity to sin.

One of the elements that is so dangerous about this belief is that it is teaching women that they should be self-sufficient and successful at all times. If a woman believes she has everything inside of herself that she needs to thrive, what does she fall back on when she continually fails and comes up against hard times, despite this ardent belief or wish that she should be doing better? This line of thinking unravels and leads to depression and, eventually, self-blame. She might think, "There must be something wrong with me. These other women are out there living their best lives and they subscribe to this ideology, so where is my big break? I'm trying so hard to search within, and I'm coming up short. I must be empty."

This leads to the jealousy monster. When other women are doing better than we are, we tend to wince and hesitate to become their cheerleaders. Though the Bible says to "rejoice with those who rejoice" (Rom 12:15), it can be a hard thing to do when filled with envy and personal devastation. I've been there, and I still fail at this more than I'd like to admit. Haven't you been there too? Ever begrudgingly commented on or liked someone's post announcing their big news, only to be grinding your teeth with annoyance the whole time? You want to be happy for them, but it's difficult when they're getting opportunities you aren't. Or maybe you can relate to being a little bit satisfied when others fail or go through difficult times because it makes you feel better about yourself. These are ugly realities we must contend with. Sound familiar?

Of course it does. We're all sinners. But there are certain things we can do to safeguard against this attitude, beginning with rejecting the notion of "inner wholeness and prosperity." At the risk of sounding harsh, I must say this: the notion is utterly ridiculous. As Christians, we should know that we are sinners saved by grace, not of ourselves, lest anyone should boast (Eph 2:8). Ladies, please hear me: if you subscribe to this ideology of "inner wholeness", you are putting Christ in a corner and believing you can be whole of your own merit, when nothing could be further from the truth. I would even venture to say that actively believing and practicing this ideology can lead to a form of idolatry—you are placing yourself above God and attempting to rely on your own strength instead of his.

This is one of the problems I ran up against when I was a feminist. I had a hard time reconciling the "inner strength and wholeness" I was supposed to have with the concept of being a depraved sinner who can do nothing apart from Christ. These two beliefs constantly conflicted in my life and led me to a state of confusion. I even started to bristle against Scripture that addressed women in a way I deemed inferior, wondering if God really got that right—a form of idolatry, placing my judgment higher than God's and worshipping myself without realizing it. Yikes. I wrestled with this for quite some time, and it wasn't until I was married that I started to realize how dangerous my beliefs had been.

Idea two: Women don't need anyone else to make them happy

Notice how this goes hand-in-hand with the previous concept. If a woman has everything that she needs within herself to thrive, then why would she need anyone else to make her happy? Again, this idea is appealing for many reasons. Life would be pretty easy if we could all walk around with the glow of self-fulfillment, never needing to look anywhere else but within for satisfaction and happiness. That simply isn't reality, though. When I take a deep look within myself, I am scared at what I see. I definitely do not feel a sense of fulfillment through any source besides Jesus. Feminism would classify this as weakness, but I call it strength. I often hear women gloat (or try to convince themselves) that they "don't need a man," but I am here to say that I desperately need a man, and his name is Jesus. So do you.

Considering this on a basic level, if we were all constantly contented with ourselves, life would be pretty lonely. True self-contentedness would lead us to selfishness and isolation, because we would no longer feel the need to connect with others in a meaningful way. I imagine that we would all sit around seeking the good of ourselves and constantly patting ourselves on the back.

This leads to another avenue of discourse. There is a difference between the idea of self-fulfillment that feminism promises and the idea of self-love. I am in no way trying to minimize the importance of a healthy version of self-love. We are made in the image of God and should show reverence towards ourselves as such image-bearers. The two greatest commandments are to love God and love our neighbors as ourselves (Mark 12:30–31). The second part of the commandment includes an implicit understanding that we all should love ourselves and respect the lives that God has given to us. Self-love is not a bad thing.

What is bad is how the world has interpreted the idea of self-love. Self-love has become a command that is often misconstrued. People tend to equate loving themselves with self-indulgence, and this is where the danger is. If you were to type in "self-love" on a social media platform, you would probably see various forms of people "treating themselves" with material pursuits. For example, many people consider shopping sprees as a form of self-love. Many people consider eating or drinking as a form of self-love. There are those who consider spa days and pampering as forms of self-love. Some consider extended periods of rest as a form of self-love. Some might even consider drug use as a form of self-love.

Are all of these things always bad? Not necessarily. Maybe the person who went on a shopping spree for some fun has been saving each paycheck meticulously and this is the reward. Eating and drinking are not bad things in and of themselves—in fact, food and drink sustain life. It is nice to have a spa day every once in a while, especially to destress. Who isn't a fan of taking a nap? And last but not least, maybe the person using drugs is doing so medicinally as advised by their doctor.

However, I'd be willing to wager that most of the time the previous conditions are not met when people go on these "self-love" benders and participate in such activities. There is an empty void inside of each person, male and female, that constantly screams, "Fill me! Fill me! Fill me!" In order to appease this void, people seek out earthly pleasures to shovel inside of themselves, hoping that they will feel satiated for once. But it doesn't work.

Why doesn't it work? The void inside of each person is a longing for another place because we were made for another place—heaven. I don't think we will be truly satisfied until we get there, but there are better ways to fill the void in the meantime, like time spent with God in prayer, worship, etc. We are told to meditate on what is "true, noble, just, pure, lovely, of good report, virtuous, and praiseworthy" (Phil 4:8–9). These things will help plaster up the void inside, not earthly pleasures that are ultimately driven by lust and consumerism.

Something I often reflect on is why, if women don't need anyone to make them happy, do they constantly feel the need to flaunt themselves and be validated on social media? The pursuit of validation, often beginning with flaunting of some sort, is an admission in itself that the praise and recognition of others is needed to feel content. In short, other people are, indeed, needed in order to make these women happy, contrary to the original claim. Some of the staunchest feminists I've seen have fallen into this cycle of contradiction without even realizing it.

What do I mean by "flaunting"? Just think back to your Instagram feed. How many women have posted recently highlighting either a new outfit, a new makeup look, or their bodies (or maybe even all three at once)? Feminists would be quick to retort that this has nothing to do with the opinion of others and is merely a form of self-expression and self-empowerment. Okay, then why did the woman who posted feel inadequate when she didn't receive a certain number of likes? Why did she feel slighted when that one person did not like or comment? Why did she start comparing herself to the other women on her social media? Why did she begin second-guessing her attractiveness and even her worth after obsessively analyzing the post she made? I'm waiting for an answer.

. . . And I'll keep waiting for an answer, because I don't think there is one that supports the feminist point of view here. Feminism is making women feel bad about themselves all while claiming to be something that makes them feel whole. It's a deadly deception.

If women don't need others to make them happy, then what about the women who claim to be feminists and are in relationships? If we're going to stick to the same line of reasoning, how do you think a woman's partner would feel if she said, "You neither add to nor detract from my happiness. I really don't need you, but it's fine with me that you're here, I guess." Just mull that one over.

It's preposterous because it can't be true. Why would anyone be in a relationship that neither adds to nor detracts from their happiness? I don't even know if such a thing is possible in an intimate relationship. The kind of relationship that neither adds to nor detracts from my happiness sounds like the kind of relationship I have with my mailman. It's neutral because he's just my mailman—nothing more, nothing less. I don't know him on a personal level.

The same can't be true of an intimate partner. You either stay with your partner because they add to your happiness in some way, or you leave because they detract from your happiness in some way. Therefore, I'd like to challenge any feminist who says that she doesn't need anyone else to make her happy to take a long, good look at her personal relationships.

This can be applied to family and friendships as well, not just intimate partners. Taking a look at my own life, I certainly don't keep my family around because they neither add to nor detract from my happiness. On the contrary, I love my family, and I think my life would lose a lot of its meaning without them. Same thing goes for my friendships. So please, let's toss out the notion that women don't need anyone other than themselves.

Idea three: Women can do everything that men can do

This one might sting a little.

Feminists believe that men and women should be treated equally, and the reason for that treatment stems from the belief that men and women are physical, mental, and emotional equals. Instead of advocating for equal treatment based on the fact that men and women are human beings with unalienable rights, feminism goes a step further and says that men and women are essentially the same and their roles are interchangeable. This is inherently false.

Let's go back to Genesis to begin this topic:

> And the Lord God caused a deep sleep to fall on Adam, and he slept; and he took one of his ribs, and closed up the flesh in its place. Then the rib which the Lord God had taken from man he made into a woman, and he brought her to the man. And Adam said: "This is now bones of my bones and flesh of my flesh; She shall be called Woman, because she was taken out of man." (Gen 2:21–23)

Adam was created first, completely distinct from Eve. To offer a companion to Adam, the Lord created Eve from Adam's body— a separate and distinct being made to complement him. If Adam would have been satisfied with another just like him, the Lord would have created another man to serve as Adam's companion. He did not do that. Instead, he knew that Adam needed a woman.

As mentioned earlier, Adam and Eve were clearly given different skill sets and callings. The Lord gave Adam dominion over the creatures, and he gave Eve the ability to bear children. Men and women are intrinsically different, which has been made clear from the beginning of time. To say that women can do everything that men can do is fallacious when considered at even the most basic level. Can women father children? No. Can men bear children? No. At the most fundamental level of physicality, men and women are unique.

The differences don't stop there, though. I believe it is apparent that men and women are different emotional beings as well, and this largely stems from the differences in their physicality. Men are naturally stronger than women and have an easier time gaining muscle mass. It may be annoying, women, but it's a fact. Take it from a woman who spent a year lifting weights and maintaining a high-protein diet, only to still struggle to do a pull-up while my husband could effortlessly perform multiple on command (without training the way I was, might I add). It's frustrating at times, but we have God-given physical limitations. These limitations don't make us any less worthy; they just make us more distinct.

The strength men enjoy can be traced back to the charge given to Adam in the Garden of Eden. The Lord told him to have dominion over the creatures and the land. Granting men physical strength to carry out this command makes sense. Men were called to be leaders from the beginning, so it is only natural that they received physical attributes to complement their calling.

We haven't been left out though, ladies. God made us unique and distinct as well. Our bodies are beautiful vessels that possess the God-given ability to sustain life. Men definitely cannot do that. From menstruation, to ovulation, to conception, to pregnancy, to birth—our bodies are capable of some miraculous feats. Our bodies also complement the bodies of men perfectly, making intimacy within marriage a beautiful thing.

Because women were given the role of nurturers, it makes sense that our emotional tendencies would be different from men. We have a maternal instinct that makes this so. Women tend to feel things on a deep level and be very in tune with their emotions and the emotions of others. This is not a bad thing at all. I believe it makes it easier for us to love our neighbors as ourselves, since we are able to sympathize and empathize deeply.

Despite these natural differences, we all have a free will—we can choose to reject our callings and attempt to change our emotional composition. Doing so, however, is going against the will of God, and it never ends well when we pit our wills against God's will. There is much confusion in the world today because people are struggling against their anatomy and biology.

Let's run through a few scenarios. Imagine that there is a woman who desires to be the leader of her household, replacing her husband. We know that God's will is for men to be leaders, especially of their own homes. However, this woman and man have decided they want to try to switch roles. How do we think this is going to go? Sure, they're "free" to do so, but it is a choice that goes directly against the will of God, which always has consequences. This couple may decide that it works at first, but there will eventually be a breakdown in this relationship. With the woman calling all of the shots, the man will be ostracized. If there are children involved, the caretaking roles will likely get muddled. We could go on and on down the list.

Imagine that there is a woman whose only desire is to be as strong as a man. She can lift weights, eat right, and maybe even resort to supplements or steroids and achieve the strength of a man—but at what cost? Eventually, that lifestyle will wear down on her body and cause her health issues. Why? Because her genetics are working against her.

Please don't misunderstand me. By giving the previous examples, I am not attempting to claim that women can never lead, men cannot be emotional, or that women cannot be strong. There are things in my own life that would contradict those claims. I consider myself a leader (in certain roles and environments), I know plenty of men who maintain their masculinity while showing emotion, and I seek to strengthen my body and defend it with martial arts. No, I'm not condemning these things. I'm simply attempting to demonstrate that extremes are not good, especially when they go against God's design. We should never try to be something we are not. Instead, by embracing the limitations both men and women have, we can celebrate our wholeness.

Another avenue of thought has to do with the practical application of "women can do everything men can do." Even if this was the case (which I don't believe it is), *should* they do everything men can do? Feminism attempts to popularize this idea by praising women who work full-time while raising children, are the primary breadwinners in their homes, and still stay on top of domestic duties (cooking, cleaning, etc.).

Women, hear me loud and clear: this is a trick. If you truly believe that being in the aforementioned circumstances is preferable, you are being worked to death by failing to embrace a primary part of your calling as wives and mothers. You are being brainwashed into thinking that constant stress, toil, and exhaustion are normal and even commendable. They aren't.

Let's rewind. I realize that there are women who have no option but to work full time while raising children and maintaining a home. I would imagine that they are tired and would like a break, and I would imagine they would probably tell us that it isn't easy. I know that sometimes these circumstances cannot be helped, and

I tip my hat to the women who must do it all (whether that be because of the absence of a partner, a death, an illness, etc.).

However, many times it seems that women choose to live life this way, in a constant state of being spread too thin. The praise that feminism gives to women who "do it all" also comes with an unspoken converse: shame or embarrassment on the women who don't. There often seems to be a stigma attached to stay-at-home moms. I, myself, have witnessed it numerous times: people talking about the "lazy" stay-at-home mom who only has to cook and clean then gets to do whatever she wants all day, people murmuring about the stay-at-home mom's lack of ambition for a career, people saying that the stay-at-home mom is too obsessive over her children and should get a life of her own . . . And suddenly the self-proclaimed feminists have begun tearing down their fellow women. It's ironic, but it's also sad.

I am not condemning women who work outside of the home. If I did so, I would be condemning myself—I work and I plan to continue working after I give birth (though in a part time capacity). Women certainly have callings and unique purposes outside of being wives and mothers. What I would like women to consider, however, is that if they have chosen to be wives and mothers, they must take those callings into consideration along with their mental, spiritual, and physical health (and that of their families).

I do not think it is healthy on a mental, spiritual, or physical level for women to be worked to the bone every single day. Living a life of the "grind" is not something to aspire to or praise when it causes a sacrifice of mental, spiritual, or physical health. God did not create us to be constantly ragged, tired, and burned-out. He desires that we would be whole and enjoy his perfect peace in our callings. Why, then, do some women choose to neglect their overall health in the name of being productive and successful?

Men are called to be the primary providers of the family. In my own family, we rely on my husband's income, and if I decide to work then my income is a surplus that can be allocated wherever appropriate. I choose to work part time because I love what I do, and I believe God has called me to be an educator. That calling will not change when I have a child. However, my primary callings are to be a wife and a mother. If my career ever got in the way of that or caused me or my household to suffer mentally, spiritually, or physically, I would reevaluate working for the sake of my family, and I would not feel ashamed to do so.

I know we don't live a in a perfect world where every family can survive on one income. In fact, it's becoming increasingly more difficult to do so in this economy. Not every woman has the opportunity to choose how much she works. I realize that I am blessed. I write this not to shame or upset anyone, but to cause a deep thought and stirring within. Are you prioritizing your family? Are you prioritizing your mental, spiritual, and physical health? As the saying goes, you cannot pour from an empty cup. It's hard work being a godly wife and mother, so be gentle with yourself and cut back on unnecessary work and unrealistic expectations where you can.

Idea four: Women's power is their sexuality

This one is difficult to consider, but consider it we must. We have already looked at the fundamental differences between men and women physically—this includes the sexual aspects. There is certainly power and blessing in God-given sexual relationships within marriage; I'm not debating that. What I am debating is that women somehow gain power by sexualizing themselves.

We see it all the time nowadays: women are exploited for their bodies, and sometimes they exploit their own bodies in the name of feminism. It's happening at an alarming rate, and you don't have to look far to find occurrences of it. Feminists condemn men who catcall women, harass them, and sexualize them, but they simultaneously sexualize themselves and by doing so attract this type of attention.

I am not saying that women are asking to be harassed based on what they wear. However, there does appear to be a kind of double standard in existence within the tenets of feminism. It's somehow okay for women to flaunt their bodies (whether this be through skimpy clothing or even something as extreme as nudes) but then be offended when men make advances?

Don't get me wrong: in a perfect world, women would be able to walk down the street stark naked without being bothered by men. Nothing warrants a man's sin. However, we need to be aware that we live in a fallen world. There is a reason Adam and Eve were aware of their nakedness after they sinned. Be smart, women. Protect yourselves. We should not be unnecessary stumbling blocks for anyone, and we should respect our bodies enough to clothe them in strength and honor, like Proverbs states.

This problem goes further than the way women dress. There used to be a time when women were seen as unworthy or dirty for having sex outside of marriage. This, of course, was never the way those women should have been treated. But we have gone so far in the opposite direction now that women who are promiscuous are seen as powerful and desirable. This is not the answer, either.

There is an innate flaw in logic in the way that feminists handle the sexual aspect of women. They want to be respected and esteemed, yet by callously engaging in copious sexual activity, they are the ones who are disrespecting and undervaluing themselves. It's another facet of the lie that will ultimately destroy self-image and inner peace.

Now that we have explored three primary ideas of feminism, I would like to offer alternatives to what advocation for women should look like. In the Bible, women are often advocated for in specific ways: women are honored, women are given a specific calling, and women are used for God's special purposes. We'll now look at what the Bible has to say about the roles of women.

Women are honored

Lest you think God has confined women to minor, merely domestic roles, we're going to take a look at Biblical accounts found throughout the Scripture. Women are honored throughout the Bible in various ways, and one of those ways is by the protection they are given. Think back to the previous chapters when we discussed the penalties for rape or physical harm. It was no small thing to hurt a woman, and men often paid for it with their lives. Why? Because women are honored as God's special creation.

Additionally, women are honored in the Bible for their faith and trust in God. Let's reflect on a few stories scattered throughout the Bible. Hannah was a woman of God who experienced barrenness. Imagine the pain she endured as Peninnah, Elkanah's other wife, successfully bore child after child while she could never even conceive. In an act of wisdom and dependence on the Lord, Hannah beseeched him, saying, "O Lord of hosts, if you will indeed look on the affliction of your maidservant and remember me, and not forget your maidservant, but will give your maidservant a male child, then I will give him to the Lord all the days of his life, and no razor shall come upon his head" (1 Sam 1:11). May we all be as trusting with our children as Hannah was with Samuel. God blessed her for her faith in him: "And Elkanah knew Hannah his wife, and the Lord remembered her. So it came to pass in the process of time that Hannah conceived and bore a son, and called his name Samuel, saying, 'Because I have asked for him from the Lord'" (1 Sam 1:19–20). Hannah kept the promise she made to God and brought Samuel to the temple at the tender age of three, when he was barely weaned from her breasts. I imagine that it was incredibly difficult to leave her son—the son she desired so fiercely and begged God for—at the temple. But Hannah did not falter, and she was honored for her obedience and faith in the Lord. Samuel grew to be an important judge, prophet, and priest who greatly influenced Israel.

Another woman who is honored for her faith and obedience is Rahab. We first meet Rahab in the book of Joshua. Rahab, by all accounts, was not a seemingly virtuous woman—she is described as being a harlot, or a prostitute. Despite the sin she was living in, she chose to obey and believe in the Lord in her dealings with Joshua's spies. She could have turned them over to the king of Jericho and cost them their lives, but her faith in God led her to do differently. Instead, she hid them in her home, incurring a steep personal risk to herself and her family by doing so. She was blessed for this effort. We are told, "Joshua spared Rahab the harlot, her father's household, and all that she had" (Josh 6:25). Not only that, but Jesus is a descendant of Rahab, which we learn in Matthew. Rahab was rewarded and honored richly for her faith in the Lord.

Women are given a specific calling

Throughout the Scriptures, we encounter all kinds of women from various walks of life. The Lord manages to use each of them for his uniquely purposed plan. Ruth is an example of a woman who was called to be a faithful, dutiful wife and daughter-in-law. When her husband died, she refused to flee in search of another as her sister-in-law did (which was arguably the wisest course of action for the time). Instead, she clung to her mother-in-law, saying, "Entreat me not to leave you, or to turn back from following after you; For wherever you will go, I will go; And wherever you will lodge, I will lodge; Your people shall be my people, and your God, my God. Where you die, I will die, and there I will be buried. The Lord do so to me, and more also, if anything but death parts you and me" (Ruth 1:16–17). This is a rather bold commitment for Ruth to make, considering that she and Naomi were both widows in need of livelihood. A prime way of securing livelihood was, of course, marrying. Yet Ruth refused to leave her mother-in-law, knowing the calling she had to care for her family. She would rather remain a widow than abandon her.

The beautiful thing about the story of Ruth is that she is rewarded for obeying the calling God gave her. She ends up marrying Boaz, a wealthy and successful man, and the Lord blesses her womb. She bears a son named Obed, who—wait for it—is also a part of Jesus' ancestry! By following her calling, Ruth was blessed immeasurably.

Another wonderful woman who undoubtedly followed her God-given calling is Queen Esther. As a Jew, she wouldn't have been considered as a bride for King Ahasuerus, but this was skillfully concealed. Her beauty won him over and she became a faithful wife and ruler of the Achaemenid Empire. When the king threatened to kill all of the Jews, she asked her fellow Jews to participate in a three day fast before she entreated her husband to spare them. One cannot help but admire how Esther, at such an anxiety-producing moment, took no action until she humbly made her requests known to the Lord. The petitions of the Jews were successful, and the king listened and spared them when Esther made her request known. The wicked Haman was killed instead, and Esther was allowed to write a decree protecting them. King Ahasuerus told her, "You yourself write a decree concerning the Jews, as you please, in the king's name, and seal it with the king's signet ring; for whatever is written in the king's name and sealed with the king's signet ring no one can revoke" (Esth 8:8). With her husband's blessing, Esther wrote a powerful decree that protected the Jews from assault, destruction, murder, and robbery (Esth 8:11). By embracing her calling, Esther was blessed with a happy marriage, strong kingdom, and she even managed to save the Jewish people.

Women are used for God's special purposes

The women we have learned about could all technically fall under this category. After all, God gave these women the resources and faith they needed in order to achieve his purposes (whether that be through the lineage of Jesus, saving the Jewish people, or anything else). However, now we're going to look at a few women who radically subverted gender norms to accomplish God's special purposes.

The first woman is Deborah, the only female judge. I love reading about her and the way that God used her wisdom to save lives. We encounter Deborah in the book of Judges, during which time she is one of the prominent judges in Israel. As many stories in the Old Testament begin, the Israelites are living in sin and are therefore subjected to the consequences of their sin. In this instance, that came in the form of bondage to King Jabin of Canaan. After suffering for twenty years, the Israelites turned to the Lord for deliverance, which came through the hands of Deborah.

Using her God-given wisdom and gift of prophecy, Deborah sent for a commander of Israel's army named Barak. She instructed him to fight Jabin's army (which was led by a man named Sisera), but he would only submit under one condition: that she go with him. Deborah's response is a powerful one: "I will surely go with you; nevertheless there will be no glory for you in the journey you are taking, for the Lord will sell Sisera into the hand of a woman" (Judg 4:9). The Lord accomplishes this by giving the victory over King Jabin and Sisera to not only one, but two, women.

Ever heard of Jael? Her tale intertwines magnificently with Deborah's to create the perfect ending to the story. As Deborah and Barak were advancing on Sisera's army, Sisera fled to a nearby ally and sought rest there. The Bible tells us that "Jael, Heber's wife, took a tent peg and took a hammer in her hand, and went softly to [Sisera] and drove the peg into his temple, and it went down into the ground; for he was fast asleep and weary. So he died" (Judg 4: 21). With their commander dead, King Jabin's army was weakened and ultimately defeated, leading to a period of forty years of peace.

With this victory, Deborah praises the Lord and recounts Israel's trouble, saying, "Village life ceased, it ceased in Israel, until I, Deborah, arose, arose a mother in Israel" (Judg 5:7). Notice how Deborah, the powerful judge who charged into battle, identifies herself as a mother rather than using any other title. Deborah's motherly qualities include her power, protectiveness, and the pure love she had for Israel. This warrior first identified as a mother, knowing that the two descriptions are synonymous. The Lord used two women, Deborah and Jael, to protect and preserve Israel in ways that empowered women and subverted typical gender roles. It wasn't commonplace for women to rule, fight, or kill men—yet these two were called to do exactly that to advance God's kingdom.

Last but certainly not least is Mary. God accomplished the most miraculous and wonderful thing of all through her—the birth of our Lord and Savior Jesus Christ. I often reflect on Mary and think how amazing it would have been to know her. She was a woman with such grace, faith, and patience in trials that seem insurmountable to us. Mary was a young Jewish girl who was engaged to Joseph when her life was forever changed. In Luke, we are given the account of Mary's calling and special purpose: " . . . the angel said to her, 'Rejoice, highly favored one, the Lord is with you; blessed are you among women . . . behold, you will conceive in your womb and bring forth a Son, and shall call his name Jesus. He will be great, and will be called the Son of the Highest; and the Lord God will give him the throne of his father David. And he will reign over the house of Jacob forever, and of his kingdom there will be no end" (Luke 1:28, 31–33). Imagine receiving this news in the dead of night. Mary definitely handled this better than I would have. I would have been terrified, anxious, filled with questions and unsure of the whole thing—but Mary is the opposite. The only question she asks is how this can be so since she is a virgin, and the angel swiftly answers that the power of the Holy Spirit will accomplish this. Mary is obedient and faithful from the very beginning. She answers the angel by saying, "Behold, the maidservant of the Lord! Let it be to me according to your word" (Luke 1:38). Mary's radical obedience to the Lord is something we should all strive to achieve.

Mary's obedience to her part in God's plan was tested at several points. Her fiancé, Joseph, had a hard time believing her story until the Lord made his will clear to him. Mary risked public humiliation, shame, and even death by falling pregnant without being married. Her life was forever changed, yet she remained obedient. Through this one girl, the Redeemer of the whole world was born. God uses women to accomplish his special purposes.

Chapter 5

Jesus Was a True Feminist

WHEN I READ THE New Testament accounts of Jesus' interactions with women, I am struck by how precious each moment is. Jesus understood women, advocated for women, and honored women. There are many accounts of his interactions with women, which we will now look at.

John 2:1–12 recounts a perfect example of the care Jesus showed toward women. We are probably all familiar with his story—when Jesus famously turned water to wine and saved a wedding celebration from disaster and shame. What is noteworthy about this account is that Jesus had not yet made known his presence as the Messiah in a public manner. He even says as much when his mother Mary asks him to remedy the situation: "Woman, what does your concern have to do with me? My hour has not yet come" (John 2:4). Jesus was not correcting his mother; he was simply stating that performing a miracle would be out of line with his current plan. Despite this, we know how the story ends: out of respect for and devotion to his mother, Jesus honors her request and turns the water into wine. Jesus' original plan to remain inconspicuous was not a bad one, but he was willing to listen and respond to Mary's request, much like God listens and responds to our prayers.

There are a few things to be understood here: it was customary in this culture and time period to have a wedding celebration that lasted for several days or more. During this celebration, there was naturally much food and drink to be enjoyed. Running out of wine would have been deeply shameful and embarrassing for the family of the bridegroom. It would have been a sign of thoughtlessness, lack of preparation, or poverty—all things that would have caused dishonor for the family. Mary was friends with those who were hosting the wedding, and as any good friend would do, she used the resources available to her to prevent disaster.

What is so extraordinary about this passage is that Jesus was willing to adjust his plans out of consideration for his mother. Jesus, the Messiah, the most important person to ever walk the face of the earth, cared enough for others to be troubled by a triviality like wine. He did not sulk, roll his eyes, or make Mary feel bad for asking him to perform a miracle. Rather, he performed it out of the abundance of kindness and goodness in his heart. Exodus commands us to honor our fathers and mothers, and Jesus was doing exactly that by his actions at the wedding. He loved, respected, and highly regarded Mary, and he honored her by honoring her request. He could have rebuked her or refused to perform a miracle—all these things would have been within his rights as Lord, but that is not the God we serve. We serve a loving God who is patient and kind.

Another instance of Jesus' regard for women can be found in Luke 8 when Jesus healed the woman who suffered from a constant flow of blood. The Bible tells us that she had been dealing with bleeding for twelve years and was desperate to be healed. She undoubtedly suffered greatly and would have been cut off from society due to her illness. When she saw Jesus, she had faith in him: "[She] came from behind and touched the border of his garment. And immediately her flow of blood stopped" (Luke 8: 44). Jesus inquired as to who touched him because he felt an emission of power from his body. The woman was undoubtedly afraid of rebuke, but she could not hide and fell down at his feet instead, eager to explain her reasoning.

What is Jesus' response to all of this? He could have scolded her for being so bold as to touch the hem of his garment, but instead he says, "Daughter, be of good cheer; your faith has made you well. Go in peace" (Luke 8:48). What a kind Savior we have! Notice how Jesus refers to the woman—he could have used any term, but he chose to call her "daughter," which is an intimate term of endearment in this scenario. This is a tender exchange between a faithful woman and her loving Savior.

Another precious moment can be found in John 8. The Pharisees bring a woman caught in adultery to Jesus, desiring to force Jesus into certain words and actions—but our Lord is mighty and cannot be forced to do anything. The Pharisees said to him, "Now Moses, in the law commanded us that such [adulterers] should be stoned. But what do you say?" (John 8:5). In their wickedness, the Pharisees sought to use the Lord's word against him. Jesus has the perfect response for them: "He who is without sin among you, let him throw a stone at her first" (John 8:7). This is a total mic-drop moment. Everyone who surrounded them scattered, being convicted by Jesus' words.

After the others left, Jesus was left alone with the woman. He could have privately chastised her for her sin, but he did no such thing. Grace and mercy abound again. He says, "'Woman, where are those accusers of yours? Has no one condemned you?' She said, 'No one, Lord.' And Jesus said to her, 'Neither do I condemn you; go and sin no more'" (Luke 8:10–11). Jesus advocated for a woman who had no supporters. She was a sinner in need of grace, and that's exactly what Jesus gave her. He saved her life and showed her kindness and compassion when no one else would. Once again, we see how Jesus is a true feminist.

Another beautiful story is told in John 4. While in Samaria, Jesus meets a woman at a well and asks her to draw him a drink of water. She asks, "How is it that you, being a Jew, ask a drink from me, a Samaritan woman?" (John 4:9). There had been a long enduring feud between the Jews and Samaritans, which is what the woman was referencing. Jesus replies, "If you knew the gift of God, and who it is who says to you, 'Give me a drink,' you would have asked him, and he would have given you living water . . . Whoever drinks this water will thirst again, but whoever drinks of the water that I shall give him will become in him a fountain of water springing up into everlasting life" (John 4:10, 13–14). The woman promptly asks for this living water, and Jesus tells her to go and get her husband. She admits she has no husband, and Jesus says, "You have well said, 'I have no husband,' for you have had five husbands, and the one whom you now have is not your husband; in that you spoke truly" (John 4:17–18). Jesus gets her attention and proves to her that he is no ordinary man with his knowledge of her personal life. He then reveals to her that he is the Messiah.

Why would Jesus, who had been so careful up to this point about revealing his identity, choose to reveal himself to the sinful Samaritan woman? He could have made a grand, public declaration; he could have found the most righteous man in the area to reveal himself to; he could have kept quiet when encountering the woman and ignored her altogether. Yet he chose to show kindness and interest in a woman who had long been cast aside.

From what Jesus told us about her past, it is clear that the woman was no saint up to that point. She'd had five husbands. While there is certainly a possibility she did so blamelessly, it is more likely that she jumped from man to man. Jesus even tells us that she is living in sin by being with another man while she is still married and has a husband. Despite all of this, Jesus chose to take an interest in her and show unmerited favor and kindness toward her. He revealed his identity, and she believed him. For perhaps the first time in her life, she had experienced kindness and respect from a man. Jesus demonstrates here what a true feminist looks like.

In Matthew, there is another notable encounter that Jesus has with a woman. While in Bethany, a woman came to Jesus with her most precious possession and offered it to him: " . . . a woman came to him having an alabaster flask of very costly fragrant oil, and she poured it on his head as he sat at the table. But when the disciples saw it, they were indignant, saying, 'Why this waste? For this fragrant oil might have been sold for much and given to the poor"' (Matt 26:7–9). Here is a woman who most likely lived in poverty. Out of the goodness of her heart, she brought this expensive gift to Jesus, only to be publicly reprimanded by the disciples. Jesus knows her heart, however, and responds, "Why do you trouble the woman? For she has done a good work for me. For you have the poor with you always, but me you do not have always. For in pouring this fragrant oil on my body, she did it for my burial. Assuredly, I say to you, wherever this gospel is preached in the whole world, what this woman has done will also be told as a memorial to her" (Matt 26:10–13). Jesus is quick to defend the woman who was demonstrating love for her Savior by anointing him with oil. In the culture of the time, it was a common practice to anoint bodies with oil before burial. It is interesting that this interaction takes place directly before Judas betrays Jesus and the plot to kill him unfolds. Clearly this woman had a purpose in her actions, and Jesus knew that.

Once the plot to kill Jesus begins, he suffers tremendously on the cross, enduring atrocities like beatings, mocking, and torture. Despite all of this, one of the final moments Jesus has before his death has to do with concern for a woman. The Bible tells us, "Now there stood by the cross of Jesus his mother, and his mother's sister, Mary the wife of Clopas, and Mary Magdalene. When Jesus therefore saw his mother, and the disciple whom he loved standing by, he said to his mother, 'Woman, behold your son!' Then he said to the disciple, 'Behold your mother!' And from that hour that disciple took her to his own home" (John 19:25–27). This happens moments before Jesus takes his final breath. As Jesus was suffering horribly and dying, his concern was not for himself, but for his mother. He wanted to make sure that she was cared for in his absence, which is why he told John he was now Mary's son. This is powerful stuff.

We have looked at instances with individual women, but there are also generalities to consider when approaching Jesus' interactions with women. Luke tells us that Jesus amassed a large following of women on his journeys: "And the twelve were with him, and certain women who had been healed of evil spirits and infirmities—Mary called Magdalene, out of whom had come seven demons, and Joanna the wife of Chuza, Herod's steward, and Susanna, and many others who provided for him from their substance" (Luke 8:1–3). While we often think of Jesus being surround by his twelve disciples (all men), we should not forget that there were also women who were devoted to traveling with him and serving him.

Why did Jesus allow these women to come on this journey? Why didn't he command them to stay at home and make themselves useful elsewhere? Wouldn't he have been burdened by having such a large group of companions? Nowhere in the text does it show any vexation on behalf of Jesus. He knew that these women were useful, they had servants' hearts, and they desired to absorb as much time with their Lord as possible. Notice how the text said that the women "provided for him from their substance" (Luke 8:3). This means that the women took every ability that they had and used it to serve Jesus. He did not scoff at their efforts, just as he did not scoff at the woman who poured oil on his head, showing again his deep love and respect for women.

After Jesus' death and burial, we know that he rose again. What we may not have considered deeply, however, is the fact that he first revealed his resurrection to women. Here is what the text says:

> Now after the Sabbath, as the first day of the week began to dawn, Mary Magdalene and the other Mary came to see the tomb. And behold, there was a great earthquake; for an angel of the Lord descended from heaven, and came and rolled back the stone from the door, and sat on it. His countenance was like lightning, and his clothing as white as snow. And the guards shook for fear of him, and became like dead men. But the angel answered and said to the women, "Do not be afraid, for I know that you seek Jesus who was crucified. He is not here; for he is risen, as he said. Come, see the place where the Lord lay. And go quickly and tell his disciples that he is risen from the dead, and indeed he is going before you into Galilee; there you will see him. Behold, I have told you." (Matt 28:1–7)

Out of his many disciples, why would Jesus allow his resurrection to first be revealed to women? Notice the pattern here. He first revealed himself publicly as Messiah to a woman (the woman at the well), and then he first revealed his triumph over the grave to women.

There is also the account of his resurrection in John that warrants consideration:

> But Mary stood outside by the tomb weeping, and as she wept she stooped down *and looked* into the tomb. And she saw two angels in white sitting, one at the head and the other at the feet, where the body of Jesus had lain. Then they said to her, "Woman, why are you weeping?" She said to them, "Because they have taken away my Lord, and I do not know where they have laid him." Now when she had said this, she turned around and saw Jesus standing *there,* and did not know that it was Jesus. Jesus said to her, "Woman, why are you weeping? Whom are you seeking?" She, supposing him to be the gardener, said to him, "Sir, if you have carried him away, tell me where you have laid him, and I will take him away." Jesus said to her, "Mary!" She turned and said to him, "Rabboni!" (which is to say, Teacher). Jesus said to her, "Do not cling to me, for I have not yet ascended to my Father; but go to my brethren and say to them, 'I am ascending to my Father and your Father, and *to* my God and your God.'" Mary Magdalene came and told the disciples that she had seen the Lord, and *that* he had spoken these things to her. (John 20:11–18)

Jesus could have chosen to reveal himself to anyone. He could have revealed himself to the apostles, he could have revealed himself to the men who crucified him, he could have gone into hiding and waited to reveal himself. However, we know that is not what he did. He chose to reveal himself to his dear follower and daughter, Mary Magdalene, once again entrusting a crucial moment and weighty knowledge to a woman.

Clearly, Jesus takes women seriously and honors them by confiding in them and trusting them with news of himself. Jesus showed himself to be a true feminist by advocating for and honoring women throughout the Bible. His examples are what we should base our understanding of feminism on, not modern-day misinterpretations. Jesus was a true feminist.

Chapter 6

The Proverbs 31 Woman

I HAVE SEEN MANY books exploring Prov 31. I have been to devotional groups dedicated to this chapter in the Bible, I have seen women make Prov 31 their mantra, and I have seen entire ministries dedicated to becoming the Prov 31 woman.

There is a reason that the woman described in Prov 31 is so famous and admirable. She sets the blueprint for how we should strive to be in our callings, specifically if those callings are to be wives and mothers. Let's examine the Prov 31 woman and make her what we strive to be like, not some modern-day notion of the ideal female. For the sake of context, here is the portion of the text that discusses the Prov 31 woman:

> Who can find a virtuous wife? For her worth is far above rubies. The heart of her husband safely trusts her; so he will have no lack of gain. She does him good and not evil all the days of her life. She seeks wool and flax, and willingly works with her hands. She is like the merchant ships, she brings her food from afar. She also rises while it is yet night, and provides food for her household, and a portion for her maidservants. She considers a field and buys it; from her profits she plants a vineyard. She girds herself with strength, and strengthens her arms. She perceives that her merchandise is good, and her lamp does not go out by night. She stretches out her hands to

the distaff, and her hand holds the spindle. She extends
her hand to the poor, yes, she reaches out her hands
to the needy. She is not afraid of snow for her household, for all her household is clothed with scarlet. She
makes tapestry for herself; her clothing is fine linen and
purple. Her husband is known in the gates, when he sits
among the elders of the land. She makes linen garments
and sells them, and supplies sashes for the merchants.
Strength and honor are her clothing; She shall rejoice in
time to come. She opens her mouth with wisdom, and
on her tongue is the law of kindness. She watches over
the ways of her household, and does not eat the bread of
idleness. Her children rise up and call her blessed; Her
husband also, and he praises her: "Many daughters have
done well, but you excel them all." Charm is deceitful and
beauty is passing, but a woman who fears the Lord, she
shall be praised. Give her of the fruit of her hands, and let
her own works praise her in the gates. (Prov 31:10–31)

Notice that the author starts by asking, "Who can find a virtuous wife?" (10). This is not a coincidence or a happy accident. The
author asks this because the understanding here is that virtuous
wives are rare: "For her worth is far above rubies" (10). Only rare
and valuable things have worth, and the virtuous wife is deemed as
having more worth than precious gems. Not every wife is virtuous.
That is why we, as Christian women, are called to be set apart and
strive for the virtues the world casts aside.

There are wives who do not esteem their husbands, who are
not faithful, who care more about themselves than their families,
who struggle to embrace their callings and find rest in the Lord.
We have all most likely struggled with at least one of these things
at some point. The good news is that Jesus paid for these sins on
the cross, and he provides us with a blueprint to getting back on
track in Prov 31.

The next portion of the text addresses how the virtuous wife is
perceived by her husband: "The heart of her husband safely trusts
her; so he will have no lack of gain. She does him good and not evil
all the days of her life" (11–12). A virtuous wife gives her husband
no reason to doubt her love or good intentions. She does this by

caring for him, caring for the household, and embracing her role as a wife. Her commitment to the Lord allows her to perform these duties so excellently. While considering what a virtuous wife looks like, we must also consider what an unvirtuous wife looks like. "The heart of her husband safely trusts in her" says a lot about the marriage of the virtuous wife. For those who do not have this kind of trust in their relationships, it also says a lot about them. Assuming a woman is not married to an insanely and unjustly paranoid and jealous man, there should be trust extended from him to her. The same can be applied in reverse: wives should also be able to safely trust in their husbands. How is this trust cultivated? It is cultivated through honesty, respect, and love. Does the heart of your husband safely trust in you? Do you safely trust in your husband? If not, why? The rate of divorce these days is unsettling, and many times divorce results from broken trust.

The text then goes on to describe the work ethic of the virtuous wife: "She seeks wool and flax, and willingly works with her hands" (13). One of the virtuous wife's defining characteristics is her stellar work ethic in relation to her household. As we've previously touched on, it's no easy task to keep a household perfectly in order. There is grace for our lazy days, and rest is certainly a good thing, but on the whole, we are called to be diligent stewards of what God has given us.

While the wording in the text may seem unrelatable on the surface, it actually touches on the common elements of daily life. By seeking wool and flax, the virtuous wife is described as making clothing and other goods both to cover her household in and potentially sell if the need arises. She is taking care of her household's basic needs, like clothing and covering, much like you and I do. While I don't make my own clothing and household items (more power to you if you are able to), I am in charge of making sure we have what we need. When my husband needs new clothing, I buy it. I've been buying clothes for my unborn child. These are small examples, but they speak to characteristics the virtuous wife has, which are planning and providing.

The example doesn't stop there, though. The virtuous wife also "is like the merchant ships, she brings her food from afar. She also rises while it is yet night, and provides food for her household, and a portion for her maidservants" (14–15). If you are married and/or have children, you probably can relate to the issue of planning and making daily meals. I'll be honest: I'm not a huge fan of cooking. Thankfully, I married a man who loves to cook and is willing to lend a hand when needed. On a regular basis, though, I am the one who plans the meals, orders the groceries, and cooks. It may seem like such a trifling task, but it is a necessary part of a functioning household, and it is a way we can show care for the ones we love.

Next, the virtuous wife "considers a field and buys it; from her profits she plants a vineyard. She girds herself with strength, and strengthens her arms. She perceives that her merchandise is good, and her lamp does not go out by night. She stretches out her hands to the distaff, and her hand holds the spindle" (16–19). This is an important shift in the text because the virtuous wife is now given praise for her work outside of her household. In a culture that was quite limiting to women, the virtuous wife is given an astounding amount of autonomy. Women were not typically allowed to manage finances or business propositions, yet the virtuous wife does both here. Not only does she do both: she does both well. Her success is noted in the acquisition of the field and vineyard. Her shrewd dealings demonstrate her wisdom and capability.

The latter half of the verse touches once again on her steadfastness. This steadfast work ethic is applied inside and outside of her home, and she is rewarded for her diligence. By working in this manner, she also "girds herself with strength and strengthens her arms" (17). If you ever wanted a Bible verse to support your gym habit, this is the one. Clearly the virtuous wife is seen as strong in every sense of the word. Her mind and body are celebrated throughout the text.

Lest we think the virtuous wife is consumed by her own pursuits, the text tells us that "she extends her hand to the poor, yes, she reaches out her hands to the needy. She is not afraid of snow for her household, for all her household is clothed with scarlet" (20–21). As a wife and a future mother, I can attest that it is easy to get caught up in the affairs of my household. I don't always think of the poor and the needy, but the virtuous wife makes a point to minister to them. Her work ethic and care allow her the means and disposition to be able to reach those in need. She is a wonderful picture of unselfishness. It can be hard these days to snap out of the "me and mine" mentality that so deeply pervades the world. The virtuous wife demonstrates the importance of caring for all, not just those we already know and love. She is able to give freely to the poor because she has been steadfast in providing for her household.

The virtuous wife "makes tapestry for herself; her clothing is fine linen and purple. Her husband is known in the gates, when he sits among the elders of the land" (22–23). The virtuous wife has a husband who is held in high esteem. By being known in the gates as an elder, we can easily surmise that he holds a position of power and honor. To support this idea, the text tells us that the virtuous wife is clothed in purple, which is known to signify royalty and high-standing. This is especially powerful when considering the compassion the virtuous wife has on the needy. Though she and her family are honored and elevated in status, she does not consider herself too good to associate with those of a lesser standing. She uses her ample resources to minister to others.

The text begins reiterating itself here, stating, "She makes linen garments and sells them, and supplies sashes for the merchants. Strength and honor are her clothing; She shall rejoice in time to come" (24–25). By mentioning again her business skills and strength, an important emphasis is placed on these traits. Despite the fact that she must think of worldly things like the survival of her household, she makes it a point to place the kingdom of God first. Because of this, she is able to rejoice in the time to come. Are we prioritizing God and his kingdom? Or are we getting swept away by the concerns of daily life?

One of the most piercing verses to me is the next: "She opens her mouth with wisdom, and on her tongue is the law of kindness"

(26). When you open your mouth, do you do so with wisdom? Before you utter a single word, do you make sure it follows the law of kindness? It can be so easy to begin gossiping or speaking harsh words about others. What started as an innocent discussion has now become a full-on roast session. This is not pleasing to God at all. Remember what Prov 29:11 says: "A fool vents all his feelings, but a wise man holds them back." It is foolish for us to put into words all of the sinful thoughts that run through our minds. These thoughts should instead be dealt with, repented of, and forgotten. Why would we give such unkind thoughts the privilege of becoming words? Clearly, the virtuous wife is experienced with crucifying these thoughts as they come. When we have the law of kindness on our tongues, we will also be slow to criticize and spread discord.

The virtuous wife "watches over the ways of her household, and does not eat the bread of idleness. Her children rise up and call her blessed; Her husband also, and he praises her: 'Many daughters have done well, but you excel them all'" (27–29). Once again, her diligence in maintaining the affairs of her household is praised. Note that this is more than just providing for the basic needs of her household. By looking over the ways of her household, this also includes the relationships she has with her husband and children, and the relationships they have with each other and others. In other words, she is largely responsible for maintaining a healthy marriage and ensuring that her children grow up to be godly people. This burden, of course, does not solely rest on her—her husband is the one who has the primary responsibility for the spiritual health of the household, but we would be remiss to say that the woman has no influence or responsibility.

I'll use my own life as an example of this. My father is a pastor, and growing up, my mother homeschooled me and my siblings. She was a stay-at-home mom. Did my father have a direct role in shaping who I am? Of course he did. Did he have a direct role in my spiritual formation? Once again, of course he did. However, if you think my mother did not influence me just as much, you are wrong. My sisters and I were home with her all day, every day.

She taught us, spoke with us, nurtured us, and helped us develop into the women we are today. We learned from her just by being around her and observing her, whether this be how she handled disciplining us, a stressful situation, sickness, joy, etc. My mother was a significant force in shaping who I am today. I learned by watching her.

I share all of this to say that you should not underestimate the importance of the role you play in all affairs of your household, not just practical ones. Your husband's heart should safely trust in you to manage the affairs of the household well, and that includes the influence you have on your children. Just like I was watching my mom, your kids are watching you. By following the example of the virtuous wife, we can instill the proper things in our children and know that they will rise up and call us blessed.

Notice how at the end of the verse, the husband of the virtuous wife praises her by also calling her blessed and saying, "Many daughters have done well, but you excel them all" (29). This is a tender and endearing moment of admiration between husband and wife. Her husband recognizes the blessing he has in her, and he expresses his appreciation with these words of praise. He knows how wonderful his wife is, and he rejoices in her success, knowing that her success brings him honor and happiness. This is the way it should be for us too, ladies. Although we shouldn't do things solely to receive praise, praise is a natural result of a job well done. Are you appreciated by your husband? Is he communicating his appreciation to you?

These last words of the text are often quoted, and there is a reason for that: "Charm is deceitful and beauty is passing, but a woman who fears the Lord, she shall be praised. Give her of the fruit of her hands, and let her own works praise her in the gates" (30–31). Earlier in this book, we discussed the deceitfulness of charm and beauty that our society is so obsessed with. This has always been a struggle, though the struggle has presented itself differently throughout each generation. The Bible has the final word on it, though. Charm is, indeed, deceitful. As previously mentioned, most of the "charming" things we see on social media are not genuine. Beauty is, indeed, passing. Everyone will get old, no matter how much they do to try to prevent it. At the end of the day, all we are left with is our souls. This is why women who fear the Lord will be praised, not those obsessed with worldly matters.

Like the virtuous wife, we should strive to be diligent in all that we do. By doing so, we will be given the fruit of our hands, as the text states. When we constantly sow what is good and holy, we will reap what is good and holy. We also will not have any need to boast in ourselves, because our own works will praise us, according to the text. Our actions will speak for themselves, and we will receive our heavenly reward. Let us not grow weary, but soldier onward instead, seeking to fulfill the example of the virtuous wife.

Chapter 7

Get Behind Me, Satan

EVEN IF WE KNOW that something is wrong, it is not always easy to resist it. Though I reject the errors of feminism, I am often tempted by aspects of the belief system or lulled into a stupor that puts my guard down. The reality, however, is that we must always be on guard against the attacks of the devil. 1 Peter 5:8–11 states, "Be sober, be vigilant; because your adversary the devil walks about like a roaring lion, seeking whom he may devour. Resist him, steadfast in the faith, knowing that the same sufferings are experienced by your brotherhood in the world." Now, I am not equating feminists with satanists—however, I do believe the devil uses elements of feminism to blind others and make them numb to the truth.

We aren't alone in our struggles, though. Even Jesus, our perfect Lord and Savior, was tempted by the devil on more than one occasion. Like Jesus, we can withstand the wiles of the devil, because the Bible tells us that we have "the mind of Christ" (1 Cor 2:16). The book of Luke details an account of temptation that I will share in its entirety:

> Then Jesus, being filled with the Holy Spirit, returned form the Jordan and was led by the Spirit into the wilderness, being tempted for forty days by the devil. And in those days he ate nothing, and afterward, when they had ended, he was hungry. And the devil said to him, "If you are the Son of God, command this stone to become

bread." But Jesus answered him, saying, "It is written, 'Man shall not live by bread alone, but by every word of God.'" Then the devil, taking him up on a high mountain, showed him all the kingdoms of the world in a moment of time. And the devil said to him, "All this authority I will give you, and their glory; for this has been delivered to me, and I give it to whomever I wish. Therefore, if you will worship before me, all will be yours." And Jesus answered and said to him, "Get behind me, Satan! For it is written, 'You shall worship the Lord your God, and him only you shall serve.'" Then he brought him to Jerusalem, set him on the pinnacle of the temple, and said to him, "If you are the Son of God, throw yourself down from here. For it is written: 'He shall give his angels charge over you, to keep you,' and, 'In their hands they shall bear you up, lest you dash your foot against a stone.'" And Jesus answered and said to him, "It has been said, 'You shall not tempt the Lord your God.'" Now when the devil had ended every temptation, he departed from him until an opportune time. (Luke 4:1–13)

I remember the first time I read this passage as a child. I was amazed (and a bit confused) at how Jesus, the Savior of the world, could be tempted by the devil. It gave me a sense of comradery with Jesus that I hadn't previously felt, because I knew that I worshipped a God who knew what it was like to go through the same struggles I did. I still feel that way reading this text today. We worship a very real Savior who experienced every pain the world has to offer—persecution, heartbreak, temptation, and even death. We can take heart knowing that Jesus has faced every trial we will ever face.

Let's start dissecting this text. The first part of the text deals with hunger:

Then Jesus, being filled with the Holy Spirit, returned form the Jordan and was led by the Spirit into the wilderness, being tempted for forty days by the devil. And in those days he ate nothing, and afterward, when they had ended, he was hungry. And the devil said to him, "If you are the Son of God, command this stone to become bread." But Jesus answered him, saying, "It is written, 'Man shall not live by bread alone, but by every word of God.'" (Luke 4:1–4)

Friends, have you ever stopped to consider that our Lord was hungry? He hungered and thirsted just as we do. After forty days in the wilderness without sustenance, you and I would likely have died—but Jesus was supernaturally sustained. However, he still felt the effects of starvation. He was weak, tired, and probably in no mood to deal with the devil's shenanigans.

The devil knew exactly what he was doing by tempting Jesus at such a low point. As I'm sure we can all attest, it's easier to give into temptation when we are already weakened. Ever wanted to remain true to your diet, but you were hungry, and that piece of pie was right there? I get it. Or maybe you wanted to remain sexually pure, but a temptation came along right as you were in a weakened physical state, and you found yourself yielding to it. We could plug in many examples here, but the point is this: it's easy to stand our ground when we are physically and spiritually charged up; it gets harder to do so when we are weakened.

With this in mind, there was Jesus, having gone without food for forty days, dealing with the devil's taunts. Instead of waving bread in Jesus' face, the devil defies him even more by challenging his knowledge and power, saying, "If you are the Son of God, command this stone to become bread" (Luke 4:3). The audacity of this statement is shocking. By speaking these words, the devil 1.) commands Jesus, 2.) questions his smarts, and 3.) tempts him.

Jesus could have rebuked him right then and there, but he was patient, and instead answered with the Scripture, "Man shall not live by bread alone, but by every word of God" (Luke 4:4). Jesus was quoting Deut 8:3 here, and he sets a good example for us by doing so: when we are tempted, our first line of defense should be Scripture.

The devil wasn't done with him, though. He goes on:

> Then the devil, taking him up on a high mountain, showed him all the kingdoms of the world in a moment of time. And the devil said to him, "All this authority I

> will give you, and their glory; for this has been delivered
> to me, and I give it to whomever I wish. Therefore, if you
> will worship before me, all will be yours." And Jesus an-
> swered and said to him, "Get behind me, Satan! For it is
> written, 'You shall worship the Lord your God, and him
> only you shall serve.'" (Luke 4:5–8)

Again, the audacity of the devil is jarring. The devil offers Jesus all the kingdoms in the world, which in itself is ridiculous, because ultimately, everything is already the Lord's. The devil only has control over certain things because the Lord allows it. Despite this, the devil makes this offer to Jesus, and the only catch is that he must worship him. The devil has some nerve to suggest this to Jesus, who is Lord of all. And this is where the famous rebuke, "Get behind me, Satan!" comes from. Jesus puts the devil in his place with a firm rebuke and another reference to Scripture (Deut 6:13).

You would think that the devil would get the hint by this point, but he tempts Jesus one more time:

> Then he brought him to Jerusalem, set him on the pin-
> nacle of the temple, and said to him, "If you are the Son
> of God, throw yourself down from here. For it is written:
> 'He shall give his angels charge over you, to keep you,'
> and, 'In their hands they shall bear you up, lest you dash
> your foot against a stone.'" And Jesus answered and said
> to him, "It has been said, 'You shall not tempt the Lord
> your God.'" (Luke 4:9–12)

Again, the devil is trying to get Jesus to use his power in a way that would not be fitting. Notice that the devil has upped his game in the sense that he is now quoting Scripture to Jesus. The fact that he quotes Scripture to Jesus, trying to use his own word against him, is appalling.

I especially find it troublesome that the devil chooses to quote Ps 91, which happens to be my favorite Psalm. It is a grim reminder that the devil is no dummy—he knows Scripture and will do his very best to pervert it by taking it out of context. The same is relevant in our lives. If the devil was so bold to take this approach with Jesus, how far will he go to make us stumble? It's a sobering thought.

By suggesting that Jesus fling himself off of the temple, the devil is acting as if Jesus has something to prove. Jesus has the perfect response by quoting yet another passage of Deuteronomy, saying, "You shall not tempt the Lord your God" (Deut 6:16). Plainly put, the Lord should be trusted instead of tested. We are commanded to trust the Lord, and anything that tests him is ultimately questioning his trustworthiness and goodness.

After these three trials, the temptations conclude: "Now when the devil had ended every temptation, he departed from him until an opportune time" (Luke 4:13). Notice this wording. The devil left Jesus and quit tempting him UNTIL AN OPPORTUNE TIME. The devil was not done with Jesus, and the text makes that exceedingly clear. The devil is crafty enough to consider the timing of his attacks as well—he wouldn't come back until the conditions were right for Jesus to be properly tempted again.

During these first three temptations, the devil attacked at the opportune time. As previously discussed, Jesus was hungry, tired, and in an overall weakened state. Why didn't the devil tempt Jesus when he was busy casting out demons, healing the sick, or feeding the thousands? Because the devil knew that Jesus was at his best then, and an attack would be more difficult. The text alerts us that the devil would be back at an opportune time to give us insight on how the devil's attacks work. With Jesus' persecution and crucifixion nearing, it's only natural to assume that Jesus probably began to experience more occurrences of a "weakened" state. We must keep in mind that not only was he fully God—he was also fully man, and part of being man is being affected by trials and tribulations.

The devil may be cunning, but he only has so many tricks up his sleeve. He largely works the same way when trying to tempt you and I—he targets and takes advantage of a weakness. Our weaknesses may not be as obvious or terrible as the ones Jesus experienced, but they are weaknesses, nonetheless.

I'll use my own struggles as an example. I've noticed a pattern in my temptations. They often come when I am spiritually weakened, and my spiritually weakened state is almost always my own fault. When I don't make regular time in God's word a priority, I experience the effects of weakness. I become dulled and numbed to the Holy Spirit inside of me, I am quick to judge and complain, and I sometimes go about my day and forget all about God. I hate it, but it's true.

The devil knows that when I am not in God's word daily, I am much more susceptible to attacks. I become lulled into a stupor and caught up in the things of the world. Everything I learned from the Prov 31 woman goes out the window, and I become a harsh and critical person. The devil knows this, and he loves it. He has a lot of fun playing around with me when I've lost my sense of spirituality. At my worst, I've had fun playing around with him, too. This is why we must be aware of our weaknesses and do our best to guard against them, lest we become a constant magnet for attacks.

I challenge you to identify your weaknesses. Where do you struggle? When do you find yourself more likely to give into temptation? By understanding these things about yourself, you will be more likely to prevent and withstand the attacks of the enemy, being able to proclaim, "Get behind me, Satan!" just as Jesus did. If you recall, this powerful phrase appears another time in the New Testament, and this time Jesus proclaims it to his disciple instead of the devil:

> From that time Jesus began to show to his disciples that he must go to Jerusalem, and suffer many things from the elders and chief priests and scribes, and be killed, and be raised the third day. Then Peter took him aside and began to rebuke him, saying, "Far be it from You, Lord; this shall not happen to you!" But he turned and said to Peter, "Get behind Me, Satan! You are an offense to me, for you are not mindful of the things of God, but the things of men." (Matt 16:21–23)

I can only imagine how Peter must have felt when Jesus referred to him as Satan. He was probably shocked, embarrassed, ashamed, sorrowful, and repentant. Though deserved, these words probably cut him to the core. So why did Jesus, the gentle Savior, speak so harshly and directly to Peter? After all, Peter's concern was legitimate. He loved Jesus and did not want him to be killed, just as we would not want our loved ones to be killed. Didn't Jesus know the intentions in Peter's heart when he impulsively uttered those words?

Yes, Jesus knows all. He is omniscient because he is God, after all. Jesus used such clear language here because Peter spoke against God's plan to save mankind, and he did so out of worldly concern. Peter was not thinking of advancing the kingdom of God when he spoke those words. He was only thinking of how much he loved Jesus, and what a terrible loss it would be to lose such a wonderful teacher and friend. His reasons for protesting were arguably selfish.

Jesus did not mince his words. Often times, people tend to think of Jesus as a quiet, nice guy who went around doing a lot of cool things for people. He is so much more than that, folks. Part of his character as Lord of all is that he is first and foremost concerned with love and truth. While Jesus' words to Peter may not immediately seem loving to us, a closer look should reveal our Lord's character. Why does God correct us? He does so out of love, even if the means of correction may seem severe to us at the time.

By uttering those words against God's plan for the world's redemption, Peter was sinning and was rightfully likened to Satan for the sentiments he expressed. Who wanted to stop Jesus more than anyone—more than the Pharisees and Sadducees, more than the naysayers, more than the corrupt leaders of the time? Satan, of course. When Peter spoke against God's plan, he was ultimately in agreement with the devil, which is why Jesus likens him to Satan.

Not only does Jesus liken him to Satan—he goes on to say that Peter is an outright offense to him by prioritizing worldly matters over heavenly ones. I don't know about you, but I don't want to be remembered for being an offense to the Lord. On the contrary, I want to be remembered for honoring him.

So how does this all relate to feminism? I'll tell you. When you continuously stiffen your neck to correction, harden your heart at the truth, and decidedly focus on selfish worldly matters instead of spiritual ones, you are no better than Peter was in that moment Jesus rebuked him. In fact, you may even be worse—Peter's protest was partially motivated by love for Jesus, but when you refuse to submit to authority and be teachable, your actions are motivated by pride, and pride is an abomination to the Lord.

Are you feeling some of that shame that Peter probably felt when Jesus called him out? That's okay; so am I. I still fight this battle, and I'm inviting you to fight it with me instead of rolling over and letting the enemy stomp all over you. I got tired of walking around battered and bruised, and it's time you also realize that is no way to live. Each time we feel the flicker of pride and temptation well up inside, may God give us the strength to proclaim, "Get behind me, Satan!"

Chapter 8

He Must Increase; I Must Decrease

Now that we've picked our problems apart and had a pity party over our wretchedness, it's time to act. We are not meant to stay in a downcast state, wallowing in our weaknesses and temptations. On the contrary, we're called to take up our armor and fight the good fight. John 3:30 is a verse to live by when it comes to this: "He must increase; I must decrease." But what exactly did John the Baptist mean when he said this, and how is it relevant to us today?

When John the Baptist spoke these words, he was referring to the ministry he started before Jesus made himself known as the Messiah. John was a key figure in paving the way for Christ, but he knew when it was time to step back, hence: "He must increase; I must decrease" (John 3:30). John knew that Jesus' ministry was going to change the world, and he was glad for the small part he could play in bringing it forth—but he knew that at the end of the day, the mission was to evangelize others and glorify Jesus. John knew he was not Jesus, and he made that very clear to everyone he encountered.

We should follow John's example and realize that the only good thing about ourselves is our redemption through Christ. Therefore, we need more of him, and less of ourselves. Why? Because we are tainted by sin. If left to our own devices, we would surely destroy ourselves. The only thing that makes us good is

Jesus, which is why we should want him to abound, and our own sinful tendencies to decrease.

When you find yourself tempted and tried, whether it be by the teachings of feminism or anything else in your life, you must remember that you have access to heavenly armor that will shield you from the enemy's attacks. The book of Ephesians tells us about this armor:

> Finally, my brethren, be strong in the Lord and in the power of his might. Put on the whole armor of God, that you may be able to stand against the wiles of the devil. For we do not wrestle against flesh and blood, but against principalities, against powers, against the rulers of the darkness of this age, against spiritual hosts of wickedness in the heavenly places. Therefore take up the whole armor of God, that you may be able to withstand in the evil day, and having done all, to stand. Stand therefore, having girded your waist with truth, having put on the breastplate of righteousness, and having shod your feet with the preparation of the gospel of peace; above all, taking the shield of faith with which you will be able to quench all the fiery darts of the wicked one. And take the helmet of salvation, and the sword of the Spirit, which is the word of God; praying always with all prayer and supplication in the Spirit, being watchful to this end with all perseverance and supplication for all the saints. (Eph 6:10–18)

You have most likely heard of this verse, but have you ever taken it to heart and dwelled upon the wonderful resources God has equipped you with? You, sister, are a warrior. You are a warrior for Christ, and in this fallen world, you will be given every opportunity to unleash your battle cry.

When I read this passage, I like to envision each piece of armor in all its glory. Perhaps it's the writer in me, but I love thinking of details like this. I can clearly see the truth around my waist, glimmering as white as snow but as firm as steel. I envision the golden breastplate of righteousness, and the beautifully crafted boots of peace. The shield of faith is pure silver, heavy with embellishments, but my arms find it as light as can be. The helmet of salvation adorns my head and frames my face so naturally that others cannot separate me from my identity in Christ. Lastly, there is the sword of the Spirit, and its hilt is encrusted with jewels. It flames as I wield it, ready to burn itself into the hearts of men.

Can you see it too? You are a powerful woman who is actively making a difference in God's kingdom. Equip yourself with the tools he's given you, and act like the warrior princess he has called you to be. When you do this, you will be able to see the increase of God and the decrease of yourself in your life.

Let's break down each tool that God has given us. The first thing that is mentioned is the truth that we are to gird our waists with. I believe this is intentionally mentioned first, because without God's truth, we cannot comprehend or utilize the other pieces of armor. Out of all of the armor that is mentioned, this is the piece that receives the least description. Why is that? I think it is because the truth is straightforward and never changing. When we think of a warrior's armor, we must acknowledge that it obviously functions to protect the warrior. The waist must be protected because of the vital organs that lie beneath it, and for some of us, this is also the area we will be carrying our children. By girding the waist with truth, we are sustained when the lies of the devil come at us, including the lies that feminism propagates.

If you are constantly believing the lies of the devil, check your armor. Have you girded your waist with truth? This should be your first line of defense against the enemy. The devil likes to work in sneaky ways, and he will do whatever he can to establish subtle lies in your subconscious. Do you think you're worthless? That's a lie from hell. Do you think others are beneath you? That's a lie from hell. Do you think God can't be trusted? That's a lie from hell. Do you think you must be a modern feminist to be a successful woman? That's a lie from hell. Get in the Bible and let the truth of God permeate your heart. Check your armor, because without the truth, you are extremely vulnerable.

The next piece of armor mentioned is the breastplate of righteousness. The function of the breastplate is obvious—it is to protect the heart. The Bible puts much emphasis on the heart, often using it as a way to refer to human emotional will. The Psalmist often refers to the heart: "Create in me a clean heart, O God, and renew a steadfast spirit within me . . . My flesh and my heart fail; but God is the strength of my heart and my portion forever" (Pss 51:10; 73:26). There is a vital link between the heart and the mind, which is where emotion comes in. We should, like the Psalmist, desire pure hearts and recognize that we must rely on the Lord to grant us pure hearts. It is not something we can achieve on our own, just as we cannot achieve salvation apart from God.

The Bible also gives a command concerning our hearts: "Trust in the Lord with all your heart and lean not on your own understanding" (Prov 3:5). When we surrender our hearts and minds to the Lord, we will experience peace and direction. With this command comes a blessing: "Blessed are the pure in heart, for they shall see God" (Matt 5:8). When we make the purification of our hearts a priority, we will reap the promised benefit: we will see God. He will manifest himself in different ways throughout our journeys, but one thing is for sure: if we seek purity and trust in God, he will make himself known to us and give us clear direction as we go about our lives. When our hearts are guarded, it is so much easier to see through the lies of feminism.

The shoes of peace are mentioned next. I appreciate the fact that shoes and peace go together (and not just because I, myself, feel at peace when I support my bad habit and purchase more shoes . . .). Shoes and peace together should leave a clear impression in our minds: everywhere we go, we must be ambassadors for Christ and conduct ourselves peacefully. No one wants to listen to a loud-mouthed, boisterous Christian. That is because loud-mouthed, boisterous Christians tend to do more harm than good when it comes to advancing the kingdom of God. They offend and startle people. Hebrews 12:14 says, "Pursue peace with all people, and holiness, without which no one will see the Lord." We must learn to speak the truth in love, with an abundance of peace. Otherwise, as the Bible tells us, others will not see Christ in us. When we learn to conduct ourselves peacefully, we receive another blessing:

"Blessed are the peacemakers, for they shall be called sons of God" (Matt 5:9). Let us be known, above all else, as children of God. The shoes of peace are also tied to the readiness that the gospel gives us. When we are equipped with the shoes of peace, we will be ready to do what the gospel commands and be the women God has called us to be. By ensuring we lace up these shoes of peace each day, our minds will be filled with the gentleness peace naturally breeds as well as an awareness of the need to spread the gospel. As explored earlier, the modern expression of feminism is one of self-obsession that leads to selfishness. The shoes of peace assist in keeping our minds on the bigger picture, which is advancing the kingdom of Christ.

The shield of faith comes next, and with it, there is a grand promise: when we utilize the shield of faith, we "will be able to quench all the fiery darts of the wicked one" (Eph 6:16). That means that anything the devil throws our way—any temptation, fear, lie—can be squashed immediately. Hebrews 11:1 defines faith as "the substance of things hoped for, the evidence of things not seen." There is a reason the Bible tells us to "walk by faith, not by sight" (2 Cor 5:7). There is so much more to each battle we face than what is in our line of sight. This is where the shield of faith comes in. When we panic and lose our faith, we become "like a wave of the sea driven and tossed by the wind" (Jas 1:6). If you've been feeling sea-sick from all the back and forth in your life, there's a good chance you've forgotten to equip yourself with the shield of faith. By equipping yourself with the shield of faith, you will be firm in your beliefs and in your callings as a woman. This will make it so much harder for the lies of feminism to shake up your world and make you feel unsteady.

The helmet of salvation is another critical piece of armor. The imagery here should, once again, point us to the truth: our minds should constantly appreciate our salvation and be aware of the lost souls in the world. The armor God has given us is not only there for our benefit. When we equip ourselves and take advantage of the armor, we become witnesses for Christ to others. 1 Corinthians 15:22 states, "For as in Adam all die, even so in Christ all shall be made alive." The gift of salvation is freely offered to all, and we should be deeply concerned with evangelizing others. When you embrace your role as a woman of God and stand up to the lies of feminism, your witness to others will be strengthened.

The last piece of armor we are called to take up is the sword of the Spirit, "which is the word of God" (Eph 6:17). Swords pierce and slash, and the way the sword of the Spirit works is by piercing the hearts of men and slashing away their wickedness. We are told that "the word of God is living and powerful, and sharper than any two-edged sword, piercing even to the division of soul and spirit, and of joints and marrow, and is a discerner of the thoughts and intents of the heart" (Heb 4:12). I don't know of any other weapon that can do that! The beautiful thing about the sword of the Spirit is that it is not a weapon of destruction; it is a weapon of healing. Sometimes we must be broken down to be built back up. 2 Corinthians 3:17 says, "Now the Lord is the Spirit; and where the Spirit of the Lord is, there is liberty." Ultimately, the sword of the Spirit brings freedom. When you equip yourself with the sword of the Spirit and constantly rely on God's word, you will find that it becomes easier to disprove and demolish the lies that modern day feminism promotes.

All of this armor is incredible, and you may be feeling over-whelmed at the thought of having to put it on, piece by piece, every single day. I'll be frank with you: there are days when you will feel too broken and weary to even lift a finger, let alone wage spiritual warfare. That's okay. It is on those days that you go to the Lord and ask him to gently place the armor on you, dressing you like a child who is too young to dress herself. When you come to the Lord in this manner, I think you will find that his strength is sufficient for you, even during your weakest of times.

Galatians 2:20 is my dad's life verse: "I have been crucified with Christ; it is no longer I who live, but Christ lives in me; and the life which I now live in the flesh I live by faith in the Son of God, who loved me and gave himself for me." I think he picked a good one. That verse is really what it's all about, folks. This book is intended to remove the stumbling block of feminism, so that you may clearly understand and appreciate your roles as women and focus on the edification of your hearts and minds in Christ. May we go forth into the world with our armor on, and may our battle cry be one of truth.

Index

www.ingramcontent.com/pod-product-compliance
Lightning Source LLC
Chambersburg PA
CBHW070737030726
47601CB00001B/42